The Book of All Lovers

The Story of Dyosphir and Ivalisee

The Book of All Lovers

– A POEM –

The Story of Dyosphir and Ivalisee

Bruno A. Ribeiro

All rights reserved. No part of this publication may be reproduced or transmitted in any form or by any means without prior written permission from the author.

All illustrations © 2017 Bruno A. Ribeiro
ISBN 10: 0692957820

ISBN 13: 9780692957820

for Ana

Contents

Preface · xi

Chapter I. — Our Prince · 1
Chapter II. — The Place · 11
Chapter III. — The Joy Killers · 19
Chapter IV. — The Creature Thordskree · · · · · · · · · · · · · · · · 27
Chapter V. — The Child · 35
Chapter VI. — Rose of Sharon · 43
Chapter VII. — Ivalisee · 53
Chapter VIII. — Fears · 63
Chapter IX. — In Which Ivalisee Sings · · · · · · · · · · · · · · · · · 73
Chapter X. — Ruby Vain Lake and the Trail of the Copper Beech Tree · · · 81
Chapter XI. — Words and Gusts · 91
Chapter XII. — The Flower Passages · · · · · · · · · · · · · · · · · · · 99
Chapter XIII. — The Saying · 109
Chapter XIV. — Hopes · 117
Chapter XV. — The Plan · 125
Chapter XVI. — The Sphere · 133
Chapter XVII. — Dreams · 141

Rhyme Scheme · 149
Endnotes · 151
About the Author · 153

Preface

Young and foolhardy Dyosphir and Ivalisee take their first steps in loving one another. Yet it will take great courage on their part to overcome the perils standing in their way. While the Joy Killers take advantage of the pursuit of his beloved to attack his princedom, our hero, Dyosphir, with the help of one Creature Thordskree and, later, the Child, embarks on a journey to rescue Ivalisee from the Sphere of Utmost Dreams—a realm where dreams and nightmares are trapped. He struggles to bring her back to real space-time and to live with her happily ever after, free in his Dyosphirland.

The Book of All Lovers is a tale of adventure and chivalry, a fantastic voyage in pursuit of a dream of love in which the hero must overcome self-doubt to find joy.

The first of a trilogy, *The Book of All Lovers* is also an illustrated fairy tale for adults in verse form. For aren't we all travelers on such a fantastic journey?

Chapter I
Our Prince

— Now you may say you meant to know its site...

I - 26

Our Prince

Yes, it is true
What You are about to perceive.
In more ways than a few,
Call Your faiths aside and believe.

Befallen in the ancient good times of trust,
Not such a long time ago,
Before we craved to touch the stars,
Before we knew what we now know.

Under an oath of regard and matter,
Underneath the pledge of "be no batter,"
Where the importance of the tatter
Would make neither You nor someone better.

Prior to the creation of the letter,
Beforehand it was put together,
To create words like "greed" and "envy"
That now can help some climb the ladder,
Fill up a paunch or a platter,
Till one throws up, to put it gently.

And earlier than the manuscript's invention,
The written verb, or the noun "conviction,"
The message, epistle, and the libretto,
In sum, all the choruses in falsetto,
Of any religion, creed, faith, or addiction.

Or the idyllic Shangri-La,
Northernmost places ruled by Ra,[1]
Folktales, hypocrisy, kumbaya.
Nonsense one mustn't believe, ah…

Open Your eyes, ears, and smiles
Now, before it is too late.
For this one here tells no lies.
Do not feel threatened; I use no bait.

By other values they were guided
These, who stood ahead of us,
With their acts I was delighted,
And now to tell them I've decided
Things like gallantry, respect, and plus.

Nonetheless, beyond these two are more.
Others are whom I want to share,
Mostly a love never seen before;
Don't think You know—You shouldn't dare.

Oh yes, it is all true,
And unveil it I am going to.
It all commenced in *the Place* known by few,
Later named after the One who once there grew.

Our Prince

He was no king, or emir,
The One all in silence called Dear,
Garbed, sauntered in a cloak of cashmere,
And answered by the grace Dyosphir.

Now tell me if You have heard
Any name like this one before!
For it came out of a singing bird
That is not here anymore.

And say it aloud if You dare,
A fearless one then You must be.
Shout it out through the air.
If You can, climb up a tree.

By the sides of all mortals He walked,
Full of graciousness and bravery.
With an aura of pure mystery,
Always leaving something to be desired.

Various would bow at His passage.
Some others just preferred to kneel.
Any manner of curve they could manage,
That expressed all the love they might feel.

Some said that a glimpse of His sight could almost cure.
Moreover, a touch of His finger nearly heal.
That never a soul existed so pure,
I would trade that one for my last meal.

By His side ran as if it flew
A golden dog, and sometimes two.
With gleaming coats and chest hair blue,
That warmth and balminess all overthrew.

With resilient fangs and muscles fit,
Belligerent claws—oh, if they could tweak!
At one thousand years, they hit their peak
And ran to mate at the supreme summit.

They didn't feed on flesh or meat.
They howled and cried if He was at risk.
Instead, miserliness they would rather eat,
The worst character defect a man can pick.

—There goes our beloved Mastron,
Cried the refined and the uncouth,
—The Only One we can count on
And feeds us dreams of love and eternal youth.

Yes, one could always find Dyosphir.
Thus the skies would for Him open clear,
And to cuddle Him the sun would go near,
In *the Place*, where a day could take a year,

Where every night was revered as a queen,
Whose king was nowhere to be seen,
Where a man chased a woman in a dream.
Later on, You'll understand what I mean.

For He didn't just meander from one road to another,
Since a residence of his own He had.
Full of servants that treated Him like Mother,
Volunteers who renamed Him Dad.

With more towers than one could count,
Its walls could build roads from east to west.
On every corner, He raised a fount
Of marble—that great god Nabu[2] would have impressed.

He erected it at the top of a mount,
In a location that couldn't be guessed.
Even I was held in account.
There's no way—it can't be confessed!

Now You may say You merit to know its site,
That a selfish one then I must be.
You can call me anything You want
(A heart his words nor deeds can daunt),[3]
Yet telling You this story should release me free.

And don't say, "It won't," for I know it better.
Your mind isn't that hard to read.
Places like this aren't far from us
(Neither the noble ones who still do buss).
Open Your hearts—You are much in need!

Or look into Your own soul and seek.
Some of You might have to poke and dig deep.
Imagine a place where You can curl, grieve, and weep,
A restful one where joy is, so to speak,
Somewhere between the slope and the peak
Of Your ribcage, where blood doesn't drip.

Select souls may find it, some others not.
Do not feel sad, so far only a few did—
Resilient ones, who unchained the knot,
And battled their ego and their ID.

Yet on a good path You are,
My Honorable Seeker.
Though these words might leave You scar,
As any fighter, warrior, jack-tar,[4]
I shall see if You're a winner or a quitter.

So as to know more, You must agree
To donate something of Yours as a fee.
Gold, gems, and charms, I do now foresee.
Do not insult me! I take no such debris.

Nor any promises that You cannot honor,
For Your commitment is the single sum I take.
If You need it bring along Your shiny armor
(Unless You are but just some other goner),
In case You think Your bones might break.

Our Prince

Still, don't be afraid to turn the page.
I bet Your smile isn't one too cheap.
There's no need to pretend—this is no stage.
Prepare Yourself; we are going deep.

And put all Your faiths in the horizon.
You—the chosen one—are now marked.
Search for the star, which has just sparked,
Before You take the leaves of the young hyson,[5]
Like the Great Bull that left his land and embarked
In search for the grounds of the great white bison.

Now light up all the fires You can.
Take it all in—do You feel it ascend?
Let Yourself go, for here there is no plan.
This is just a beginning You'll pursue till the end.

Chapter II
The Place

All around *the Place* they waved, the white oaks,
Curbing walls made of flat stone,
And the thatched roofs shaped by skilled folks,
With strong hands of unbreakable bone.

Same bone that forged tools from the toughest steel,
The one that sometimes falls out of the blue,
To work in any inclement conditions,
And last a thousand lifetimes too.

No soul could remember the beginning of it all,
If the first crops were harvested in the summer or fall.
How the oaks got there, no one could recall,
Or if the walls were built up during the calm or the squall.

Yet I know this one thing for sure:
That for each adversity they could endure,
Life would be celebrated joyfully.
For any illness where they found a cure,
And therefore, their fortunes reassure,
A big feast was held noisily.

Where they all ate and drank along with Dyosphir,
Sharing ageless recipes of stews and beer,
Children danced and sang along in a chorus,
Tuned throats and eyes seeking *Corvus*:[6]
—"*Coocu, coocu*"—here's to them my own cheer.

The Place

Shanties[7] of sailing the Big Sea,
On their small rafts, they sailed with thee,
In search of a place where foibles could be set free,
Away, far away from we can now see.

I'm sure You must have heard some long-dragged ones,
But if You did not, I'll gladly unmask
Their ballads of joy without mentioning guns
That came out of the deep at the tip of the flask.

About all the monsters that lived in the dark,
And their skills at riding dolphins and whales,
Not just tales, but real endeavors—I remark,
Like the one in which two friends rode the white shark,
Plus some other beasts covered in scales.[8]

Then all their talents in hoisting the free,[9]
Or about rigging the one-mastered sloop.
Flairs of privileged ones, we must agree,
Who bare-handed from the hive the honey they scooped.

The song about the twenty-man crew
That spent months at sea, above all too,
Trapped amid the high waves and the white spew,
Searching for any glimpse or a full view.

Hailing aloud from the edge of the floe,[10]
Challenging the ice as if it were a plateau,
Or standing on it, they put on the best show.
Intoning these words, I'll now whisper below:

—"*Hum, hum, hum, hum,* four times *hum,*
To those in peril upon the sea.
Don't forget next to you stands your chum,
For him *hum* again, you men of bel esprit.

"As He'll surely bring you back home,
Right to the safe of the quay,
Where you could finally rest under the dome
And sleep lying down and not on your knee.

"Where you can then sip the warmest tea,
After embracing your most loved ones,
Who kept on lulling their treasured sons,
While sighing, 'My Captain, bring them back to me.'

"Prince Dyosphir, please heal my pain!
The sight of the mast is far out plumb.
This rope is weak, and I have no chain.
Look deep in my eyes, as they're growing glum.

"You *hum, hum, hum,* this time, times three.
Don't yet spit the herb next to your gum.
Take a deep breath; tell me, what do you see?
It won't be too long before you'll get numb.

The Place

"Oh Lord, oh my Lord, I am tasting the bottom.
Sinking slowly like a red leaf in the autumn.
Burning down my last breath full throttle,
All the way deep, soon to be forgotten.

"*Hum* again, dear brother, but now only twice
For Master Dyosphir, like a mourning dove.
As your soul, He will save at any price.
You know, He's a Seeker of Utter Love.

"Thank you once more, our beloved Mastron.
I almost fell into the forgotten land.
You're still the Only One we can count on.
Here is your servant offering you his hand.

"Now *hum* one more *hum,* this time the last one,
For those who went out there and never came home.
Both forehead and hands wizened by the sun,
Dig deep, my brother; you won't find it in the Tome.

"With your last *hum,* the bells tolled, dingdong,
Declaiming all the good things that went wrong.
On behalf of these men, repeat—you're strong.
If you don't know the lines, just *hum* me this song."

In moments like these, He would give them a word.
One of those facts that rarely occurred,
For most of the time, to listen He preferred.
I saw it too, and this is what I heard:

—To each one of you, I raise my cup.
I am here for you, you utmost honorable people.
By this bonfire, I now stand up,
Embraced by the stars at the top of the steeple.

It was thanks to all that we've gone this far,
But we mustn't forget that danger never sleeps.
We will stay altogether and prize who we are,
Right before finding and climbing all the peaks.

My thoughts are with you a thousand times above.
The rejoicings we've accomplished make me so proud.
Yet we're still on this pursuit for Utter Love.
On that behalf, now before you I bow.

Tonight I will also discourse about
Something you want to know for sure.
Yes, I sense your doubts and fears.
You've so well hidden behind those cheers.
We know our innocence is not that pure.

The Joy Killers' aura you sense is real.
For a glimpse to attack, they all await,
But we must, at all cost, conserve our vigor,
To prevent their feasting on us in that wrong rough rigor.
We've been through this before and must keep up our faith.

The Place

You are my people; I hail you the most.
Together we've drifted from coast to coast,
In searching for places of the innermost.
I hope you see me as a good fellow and host,
Someone always present, not just a ghost.
To us growing old together, I'll now make a toast.

So let's sing and dance as the ones before us did.
It's because of them that we are all here.
Let's keep ears and eyes open to avoid any skid,
And always remember to hold sharp the end of your spear.

Then everyone raised the cup and toasted:
—Long life to Dyosphir, our Lord and protector!
The children stopped playing; then in unison shouted
Some name I can't recall, but like God it sounded,
As if He had been their own mighty creator.

Afterward they all retreated to their homes.
I could hear in the air some still intoning the tones.
Then fires were stoked to warm up the bones,
Inside those strong walls made of flat stones.

Their right and left eyes alternated to wink.
I saw clouded beliefs coming up little by little,
Until some shades of fading blue with hints of pink
Slowly killed the moon again, making them blink,
And announced new smiles in the morning spittle.

Bringing bliss and surprise, two gifts oft despised.
Enthusing about the community tasks and responsibilities,
For a new day had just arrived,
Where they could share all their abilities.

Rising every morning was always so pleasing,
So were those skies where flocks of slow birds flew,
Cutting all the white-seeded clouds into two.,
Much to our bliss, I assure I was no longer sleeping.
Don't say a word, or You'll blemish it. *Shoo*!
I wish You could've seen it—all that gleaming…

Beaming on their unaware innocence,
Chained against something not so pure.
In the air a feeling of a certain impotence
Torments that one must, at all cost, endure.

Chapter III
The Joy Killers

Argh, His gut sobbed
In the middle of the night,
As if it had been robbed
From its life-or-death bite.

—Our Prince suddenly cried!
Shouted the servant, the adviser chief.
—Bring all the help you can find.
Any inkling is welcome, but be brief.

—We beg your pardon? Highest volunteer helper,
You know we're here to serve our Mastron better.
He provides our families all the food and shelter,
While looking after both the young and the elder.

—A name again I've heard!
The servant's chief lastly whispered.
Among the help they shouted:—What?
A second time and a third,
He then repeated the word.
—We are in trouble—he thought.

—I, Dyosphir, just saw this cold desert!
There is no turn away or avert.
Among the staff they tried a "shush,"
Then mumbled something like ambush.
—We can't allow our Ruler again to get hurt!

The Joy Killers

—Tell us what it is, Master!
As we feel our world is about to shatter.
Let us know more about Your dream's laughter!
This'll bring us nothing but disaster.

—I can't believe you need me to repeat!
From the gut, He once again sobbed,
In an effort to make ends meet,
As if of His heart, He had been robbed.

—I won't say this again!—Dyosphir held.
All I know is her grace: Ivalisee.
She's someone whom with me you should worry to wed,
If you don't want to get yourself dead,
Before the Joy Killers bring us the disease!

—It's a dream, Master, again one we can't understand.
Your words and troubles do not make any sense.
We feel ourselves lost, rowing in strand,
Altogether confused in a mist way too dense.

Dreams are, pardon, my Prince, kin of death,
And with it, they'll always be in debt.
One mustn't worry, never ever, about that.
Just let us help You to soften Your breath.

—You all mock me and question my word?
Or fear that my vision got blurred?
—Never, Master, with Your views we'll all be on board!
—By no means, that's not what I've heard.

—I must go out right now on this quest!
One to save both the lady and ourselves.
Shall I make it to the east or the west?
What should I bring off my shelves?

Please find it out, and let me know!
Dyosphir said, faster than they could foresee.
Altogether they ran, from the ones atop to below,
As busy as a diligent late-Autumn bee.

—But, Master, You're having these dreams again…
Reminded the head servant, hiding a tear.
—It is not the first time this year.
I still remember day one, way back then…

—As limpid as this, I have never seen afore.
But above and all, I understand your fear.
She is someone I sense I adore.
Help me out to pursue her or get near.

—I'd say today His words revealed more,
Later noticed one of the staff with sharper mind.
—I find this is something we should go for.
Some others repeated—What did you find?

The Joy Killers

—We've heard the name, definitely a *she*.
Up to that point, we all agree.
But there were times the dream brought him a *he*
Whom He also wanted to go set free.

Plus a name came up for the first time,
One too hard to forget: Ivalisee.
She's trapped in a desert, and we don't know the clime.
This is no revelation we couldn't foresee.

But the Joy Killers shouldn't again be cited,
As they bring us nothing but heart emptiness.
That dreadful spark can't again be ignited.
For it might take us back into darkness.

We are the most respectable disciples.
Continuing to obey our Mastron, we pretend.
I advise we stop running in circles
And instead follow Him again till the end.

Furthermore, I will say
That once more danger is out and here today.
I suggest we face it with no more delay.
Hands on, companions; let's wake up, hey!

—You have spoken well,
Another fellow held.
—For less than this, in the abyss we almost fell,
But my belief tells me that this could be a spell.

The council continued way into the night,
Where they debated what for Him was better.
Now You must be asking if they had the right!
Such frivolous thing as "right" here has no matter.

As Dyosphir always had the last word,
One that for Him was way too clear.
Though for others it could've been absurd,
He would not give it up in a year.

So what do we have here now?
I ask You, my Attentive Reader.
Second question: tell me how?
Though I might be in need, You are still the needier.

Although, if I had known, I would say so,
I'll reveal You something, My Dear Friend
(Nonetheless, the facts are yet to come),
Take a wild guess: a love delayed and numb,
One we don't know if to defy or to defend.

I'm sure You've felt one like this before.
Well, if You haven't yet, then maybe tomorrow.
Since there's a place on earth for You,
A special one reserved for few,
The ones who didn't and don't feel sorrow.

The Joy Killers

Because the limit of the line,
The misleading one that You did find,
Plus all the others together combined,
Is way distorted and undefined.
The cruelest one of any kind,
To understand it You will go blind.

Nevertheless, seek it at any cost,
Even if You think it might not be.
I gave it up once. I got lost.
Today life has sucked the time out of me.

Now go get it, and let me know.
I'm sure You'll make it farther than I did
While alone You'll need to go.
Not in a hurry, one must push slow;
It is on You I've placed my bid.

Alive I'll try to preserve the flame,
For this is not a losing game.
To me You must bring back the Name,
And put the faithless ones back to shame.

I'll do my best to keep up with You.
In the meantime, these words I will set free.
This is a mission You must go through,
Something that You always knew,
Like Dyosphir's love for Ivalisee.

To conclude now, I'll let You know,
What the council decided at the end:
They shouted, "Our Mastron we must follow!"
And patiently waited for his command.

But what the dream did not tell
Was which direction they should go.
A snowy desert could be cold.
A sandy one at night as well,
So He repeated:—I must push slow,
And in a deep sleep again He fell.

There was no other way to find out
Other than to plunge and follow the stream,
Wishing that it brought Him another vision about
Ivalisee, or maybe a gleam.

Chapter IV
The Creature Thordskree

From pure sound came out purest silence,
Which echoed from endless mountains.
A muteness one could hear at a distance,
Snaking across the valleys and canyons.

The smells of resin and honey,
And an austere, lucid intoxication
Took over our Prince's mind,
Bringing Him nothing but frustration.

His voice again climbed the steps
And mumbled something overly complex,
Leaving all the servants perplexed,
Reminding them about living under the hex:

—Tell me why I can dream no more!
I'm dripping sorrows from every pore.
This is something I don't recognize,
As it is not mine anymore.
I feel my throat is way too sore.
I am too exhausted; I can no longer be wise.

Through the servants permeated a chill,
One of those that could almost kill,
Bringing them to a freezing stillness,
A close reminder of some heart illness,
Typical of any Joy Killer's will.

The Creature Thordskree

Of which some distinct servants experienced the presence,
   Brought by that conveyor breeze of essences.
     Felt by others in previous sessions,
   But only the ones with sharpened senses.

    So *Asclepius*[11] they summoned,
    To take Him into the *Abaton*[12]
And help Him again to dream about that woman,
     So as to end that depression.

     For a signal they awaited,
    In their innocence and purity.
     Only to find out, frustrated,
   Something we all knew and hated:
      The god's own impunity.

    But the men didn't quit at all,
   A prerogative You should remember:
    Always run away from the banal,
    The first ones You must dismember.

      And an idea came up
    To one of them in the bunch,
      Almost like a hiccup,
That they toasted to with spicy punch.

Then a challenge was announced
That could neither be wrinkled nor trounced,
Which would pay off, therefore didn't bounce.
Thus, all around it was pronounced.

One to help Him lie down and dream,
For which some assistance they gathered.
Then the council assembled up a team,
And a plan was then bartered.

To travel all around *the Place*
And spread the word at every corner.
It was no walk but a fast race,
Well prepared to make no mourner.

They opened all the closed shutters
And raised every blind stone.
No soul was left out alone,
Out of doors or inside structures.

—Together we should rise and never bow!
Shouted those in long red cloaks:
—All our strengths we must unite now!
They continued screaming to all the folks.

—Dreams we must bring back at any cost
To our Mastron's mind, so His heart can heal.
We need to mend His feelings, so they won't be lost.
Enemy is imminent; that's what we feel!

The Creature Thordskree

And yet they cried and called as needed,
Right after each honorable one was greeted.
Everywhere they went these words were repeated:
—We shall last forever and won't be defeated!

It was like this for thirty days or so,
After which all eyes stared at the ground.
In spite of that, they refused to accept the "no,"
But the "yeses" were nowhere to be found.

Deeper became the hollows in their faces,
Darker the darkness they knew.
Of the shimmering light, no one found traces,
And there was nothing else they could do.

Then suddenly it happened,
Between the mists of mystery,
In a way we'll never understand,
Though it be written down in history.

Like those things in space-time,
Materialized by the sublime,
Credited to the divine
(And these performers of mine)!

Or a breeze in springtime,
Fiery heat cracking the cone pine,
Plus the faultless size of the tide,
Altogether combined.

An old Creature approached the men,
Pointing out toward the woodland.
Their red cloaks, which were no more than ten,
Once graciously composed, commenced to fan.

—One thing for the other, you must sacrifice.
And of not protecting your leader you won't be accused.
The Creature's words came out at a price,
Which got the men way too confused.

—If you desire, I'll take you to where he is.
The only who can assist you now.
I can get you there in a whiz.
Will even lead the way, if you allow!

The Creature had no nose or eyes,
And ears were nowhere to be found.
Instead of walking, he zigzagged,
Carrying in his type of claw some little bag
That he pulled and dragged over the ground.

All the cloaked men looked at one another,
but silence was all that came out of their mouths.
It was a moment they wished they could speak.
When the Creature took over again and squeaked,
His good intentions out of his maw,

The Creature Thordskree

The oxen stopped tilling the fields,
Butterflies detained their wings,
Soldier bees laid down their shields,
And the sixth planet freed his rings.

But the men simply responded with a shrug
That summarized all the answers in the world.
Next, they all drank from the jug,
Giving the Creature a good whirl.

—Let's see if you still know where to find him:
This so-called only one who can help us now,
So should you be so grim,
No fortune could save you, no vow.

But the Creature wasn't troubled,
Nor did anyone there see him crumble.
Instead, the given dose he doubled,
Bringing all the men down to a puzzle.

For where they saw no enmity,
Therefore, he was given a last advice:
That in case of perjury,
Whatever was his destiny,
He would pay for it at a great price.

—What type of being are you?
A red-cloaked man with a calmer voice asked.
—That came out of the blue
And through no breach so easily passed?

—My name is Thordskree.
In case you have no further question,
Pronounced the Creature with a guileless expression.
—So it was my father's name before me,
And a score of fathers earlier, for your discretion.
The most loyal servants you'll ever see.

Now do you really want to be free?
He probed, extending his sort of claw,
As if to say, you should come with me,
To the Child I'll take you; follow!

Chapter V
The Child

"Nine four to the west,
Three two to the south,
I shall not stop or rest,
Nor will I open my mouth."

Thordskree—the old soul—showed the road
To the red-cloaked men of doubt,
While in silence they freed their questions,
Unable to scream or shout.

And he led them through the clears,
Deprived of his eyes and ears.
While his followers dropped uncertain tears,
Of fear, and of fear of older fears.

That they profusely washed away,
In the near waters of a *Speaking Bay,*
Which three of them it stole to depths so deep
That they could not find a way
Back to the surface that day,
Lost forever in profound sleep.

Making the other men so mad,
That they all demanded the head
Of Thordskree on a plate
Right away before it was too late,
The only thing that would make them glad.

The Child

While the speaking waters became silent,
As in: "That's enough; be quiet!"
The red cloaks became less violent
And ended up the imminent riot.

The Creature then enquired of them
About the pledge they had made before:
—Things like this will happen again,
Up to when you will be less than four.

But still they kept closing the ring
Around Thorskree, who then sustained:
—This is no time for an abrupt fling.
To a quest, courage a man must bring.
If he doesn't have it, then he should be ashamed.

—Plus, you dare to question my acts?
I thought you were all men of honor.
Remember that everywhere there'll be traps.
Should I keep guiding you to the Child, I ponder?

The men then quieted but requested
For the calmer one in the group to lead,
Since that turn they'd already regretted,
When, from his calm voice, the one stepped down and said:

—Will our acts you reconsider?
You Creature of gallant vigor,
Your utmost noble manners and figure,
We admire while approving your rigor.

Our will to go on this quest is greater
Than everything else combined.
Among us there is no traitor
Or defector of any kind.

—I do, said Thordskree, acknowledge your regrets.
But you must be strong, as this will ache.
What your tired mind now forgets
Is that over *the Bridge* only one I can take.

And he finalized by saying:
—I'll rest now, but I should be awake,
When I find a way that meets our fate.
You must do the same while waiting.

On the third night of the third moon,
To find his direction he managed.
Some didn't expect it to be that soon.
They had to leave the time the tide ebbed.

The red cloaks then followed the Creature
Into the *Woodlands of the Truth,*
Which all the men's natural features
It figured out like a crawling sleuth.

The Child

Bringing out their old doubts and fears,
Hidden behind those previous tears,
For more than so many years:
—"Once in *the Woodlands*, your self-truth appears."

That they tried to spook away,
Humming together, to Thordskree's despair,
Their utmost favorite refrain,
Which echoed throughout the air.

And woke up a drowsy whirl
From a nap of ten existences,
Which against the trees it hurled
The men to unreasonable distances.

—Be silent!—Thordskree ordered,
When three of them lost both their legs.
Next, their vanishing he watched in horror,
While the other four cried their begs.

Toward these he threw a rope,
Which ultimately restored some hope.
Thence out of his bag, he took out a globe,
Which brought light within a scope.

Calming down the *Woodlands'* wrath,
The globe lit up an aftermath,
Revealing the dimension of the bloodbath,
Prophesying new encounters along that path.

—We demand protection, one man shouted.
Our safety, you're not bearing.
Of you, Creature, we've always doubted,
We are weary of hearing your swearing.

—You should keep quiet, Thordskree warned.
Although all you do is cry,
I admit I'll be surprised,
If at the end you find your rye.

In defying me you've specialized,
When the rule was to obey.
You've ignored me when I advised.
Now we move along, I say!

Again the cloaked man in his calmer voice
Approached the old Creature and declared
That they would follow him to the ends.
Next, he asked him for his pardon and to be friends.
Plus that without him they all be condemned.

Now You might be wondering, my Honorable Reader,
To where the other six men might have gone.
They went to heal the trust in their spirits,
Through the revelation of their most hidden secrets.
I know that You might think it's in vain and bygone.

The Child

Nevertheless, there's always a decision to make
In matters of what to give or take,
Or in the futile old subject, "Make or break.,"
Go ahead, as You know, I still in You have faith,
Though all those matters are just a mistake.
This is just their story, one You might think is fake.

Therefore, the four red-cloaks continued their way,
Led by an old Creature whom some of them doubted,
But, as the calmer one in the group would say,
His utmost noble manner some thought dour.

In pairs of two, the men walked through the clears,
Behind Thordskree, when they first saw *the Bridge*,.
Guarded by a sizeable dog with perked ears,
The biggest one they had seen in years,
Who toward them ran, jumping over a ditch.

The dog barked out loud all his sadness,
A dull alternative to a well-hidden happiness.
His tail he waved in cheerfulness,
But apparently some knees confused it with badness.

The four knees of the men in the back almost spewed,
The same time their other bones started to twitch.
While the other four of a lasting twenty-knee crew
Stood their ground, for those knew what to do.
You're about to find out which were which.

As their throats wailed out loud in despair,
Those four knees of those men in the back,
Clattering, they ran away from a nightmare
That they saw on a joyful dog that wasn't even black.

And yet, two red cloaks made it for their own sake,
Plus Thordskree, who still had to decide
Which one of the two men he had to leave behind,
When the dog sat next to one, defining his fate,
By licking his foot and toenails, satisfied,
To the Creature's joy, who found out whom to take.

In all his calmness, the chosen one removed the cloak.
Thordskree and the other man dropped down a tear.
Across *the Bridge* to the Child, that one the Creature took,
And the Child said:—Welcome to me, Dyosphir.

Chapter VI
Rose of Sharon

— A Rose of Sharon is a gem that will keep your heart closed...

VI - 35

—Take me to where I should go,
For this cold blood in my veins
Is now beginning to flow,
To where I hid all my pains.

Look up at me.
You know that I am real.
—Is this true? I ask.
—Yes, I know how you feel.

—I am stuck beyond *the Sphere*,
In a place so far away and near
That tomorrow it might disappear,
If you don't come to me fast, my dear!

Our Prince recited His dreams,
All his doubts plus the night screams,
His dialogues with Ivalisee,
Which were very real, so as it seems,
Also approaching some older themes,
While the other two quietly sat on one knee.

The Child listened carefully,
Foreseeing His destiny.
Next, if they wanted to drink he asked,
When the water in the fire pit boiled at last,
As Dyosphir still debated if the Child was a he.

—You should worry about yourself, instead
Hearing Dyosphir's mind, the Child said,
—I am no woman nor am I a man.
I am something that you'll never understand.

—But let me pour down some water first,
In this deep container made of clay.
Our Dyosphir and the Creature quenched their thirst
And scrubbed the torments of a long day.

As they lay down next to the Child in the burlap,
The Child studied Dyosphir's lip marks on the cup.
Scratching the dirt with a stick, he made a map,
Making sure to leave no gap,
Holding next to his eye a small loupe.

—It's a siege, it's a siege!—the Child cried,
Waking up Dyosphir and the Creature Thordskree.
—Have neither hopes nor fears—we can't hide.
This woman is real, and You must set her free!

—My dreams are real. Is that what you're saying?
He lifted up the Child, breaking the loupe in a fling.
Then a song, He commenced to sing,
Both the Child and Thordskree surprising.

—Yes, Your suffering from her absence is real,
And You're right for not fearing the things You feel.
Though You haven't yet met her, if You want to, You will.
—It's only in dreams that we find our love ideal.

Though I just wrote the previous line for You, Reader,
I know for sure that the Child won't agree.
While Dyosphir hadn't figured out about the Child's gender,
All that mattered was the Child had the power to oversee.

Since Dyosphir was doing more than He could,
To someone who didn't know much about how to rule,
Despite being idolized, for which He had been schooled,
A smart one He grew, discreet, with the hint of a fool.

However, our Prince first doubted the Creature.
Who wouldn't? Even a pure soul…
To tell You more about Him, I'm eager,
But those thoughts now I must control.

Yet a pure soul can also be a sinner.
If You are someone who believes in those things,
Do not feel guilty; You're already a winner;
Hear me well today, and then go cut those strings!

For they were implanted in You back then,
Way before You were even born.
Do not ask me. I do not know when,
Get over it; do not be stubborn!

Once You have done it, take a deeper breath
Toward the brighter light that You now project.
It's no longer a question of life or death.
You did well, and You have my respect.

Back to the one I was talking about.
Again, do not think I don't know my own words,
For what I was doing was just checking out
If You were still keeping up with the records.

—It's a siege, it's a siege!—said the Child,
Before I interrupted the prophecy.
I apologize, for sometimes I go wild.
Now let's move on with the rest of the history:

—They trapped Ivalisee way out there,
Within *the Sphere of Utmost Dreams*!
Both Dyosphir and the Creature asked: "Where?"
The Child said: "We must save her now by all means!"

But after a better look at the lip mark,
The Child saw something hidden that hit like a spark,
Then sighed the following remark:
—The concealed monster is about to embark…

—Embark where?—held Dyosphir—If I may ask?
—On a journey that might take us back into the dark,
Where our hearts will go numb and our feelings stark.
I wish our wits were well tuned, just like the lark.

Thordskree jumped right off his knee,
While Dyosphir demanded the Child be more precise,
—They are using her as a lure: Ivalisee,
To attack Your people upon Your absence.

—But that would prevent us to continue
Our pursuit of Utter Love.
Then toward the night sky, all His fury Dyosphir threw,
For that was something He was frightened of.

—To get her out of there, we must find a way,
Stated Thordskree, capitulating before his impulses.
—That area, my friend, is way too gray,
Said the Child, so gray that it repulses.

—But can't you make it blue instead?
Interposed Dyosphir, changing to a shade with a better sound.
All three then began the following conversation,
Child, Thordskree, Dyosphir, for Your better comprehension,
In this order and not any other way around:

—I feel Your worries, Mastron Dyosphir,
But this is something that I can't do alone.
Despite the fact that I will get You closer,
And acknowledging all the love You now feel for her,
I must say that this might hurt us to the bone.

—What do you mean by that, dear Child?
That our hopes are half-beguiled?
Can they be reconciled?
Could you please bring back their smile!
Poor couple, so young and mild,
I feel my blood is now running wild…

—There must be more that we can do.
I feel I am almost touching the place,
Where we won't hold one hand, but two,
Where I'll finally feel her velvet face?

—Wise and patient, we now must be,
Though the Joy Killers want You to dream instead,
For more than one existence with Ivalisee
So that inside Your people's hearts they could see
All in Your absence—the Child said.

And added something about *the Sphere*,
Like it was farther away than it appeared.
Plus some other mumblings not so clear,
While Dyosphir wiped off a stubborn tear.

—We must trick Your heart so it can fool them!
The Child came up with a solution.
—And block hate and its resulting mayhem.
I'll be able to do it if I can find this gem,
For it will give the Killers the right illusion…

Yet You must learn how to search
Within *the Sphere of Utmost Dreams*,
Where You'll be by Yourself in a lurch,
In solitude, hovering along all the streams.

The Joy Killers are more powerful than I thought,
And made You dream about that girl.
Smart choice, she gleams like a pearl
That You might have seen once and never forgot,
Becoming all tangled up in that whirl,
Unable to untie the knot.

Now let's go search for the Rose
So that with its root I can make an infusion.
A Rose of Sharon is a gem that will keep Your heart closed.
Therefore Your feelings will be free from all delusion.

Chapter VII
Ivalisee

— It is the most perfect shape,
A man has ever seen... VII-26

Ivalisee

—Are you still with me, Dyosphir?
Do you hear my words, my beloved Prince?
Cried Ivalisee out of *The Sphere*.
—Being away from you only makes me wince.

I wish that I could take all this back,
Way back to the beginning of it all.
Please forgive me for all the pain
That I have caused you; it's all my fault!

I have no right to ask you this:
But without you, I see no bliss.
Please get me out of this abyss!
Hurry up to steal my kiss.

For I have saved it just for you,
I know you've saved yours for me too.
We are same bone and same flesh,
But both our dreams seem reduced to few.
The road is blurry; we can't see through.
Entwined are our viscera in the same mesh.

Come to me. Fly to me; I'm drowning in this stupor…
Now that we know we're real, brighter is our future.
By my side the black clouds you will blow away
So that again to your people you can show the way.
There won't be sickness or wound we won't suture.

—I hear you so well, Ivalisee,
Though out here it's still too dim to see.
I'm almost there; to you I will flee.
Do not feel sad; free soon you'll be.

Right now, I shall stop this Present
From pushing the Future into the Past
So that when it gets to the place you were sent,
The Past won't be but a shade at last.

Since I woke up one day to this throbbing lash,
An intense prelude replete with you,
I can tell that the tyrant army I will smash,
And its castle I'll put down to ash,
To build one just for us two!

—Your dreams aren't as blurry as before,
Interrupted the Child along the way.
Though Thordskree wanted to hear some more
Of Dyosphir's visions, he didn't say.

With our Prince on his left and on his right the Creature,
The Child, in the middle, knew those grounds like a teacher.
Half their size in stature, twice their weight as a leader,
A real commander in chief with no signs of a dreamer.

While Dyosphir kept thinking: Why in all the years
The names of these two never reached His ears?
When He believed He knew all His volunteers,
His Place, His dogs, His purity, and His peers.

—Busy You have been in being idolized
Came the Child in promptness.
Dyosphir shouldn't have been surprised
With the Child's wit, again, I guess…

We both have been around,
For more than two, plus one existence.
Though they call me now the Child,
I have been watching You from distance.

We are older than the older ones You knew.
Thordskree is even older than me.
Of Your fight, he has been an important key,
And with the father of Your great-grandfather he grew.

Before "the Child," I was known as "the Elder."
Back and forth I've been going around *the Place*,
Hiding here and there, wherever I find shelter,
Making any hole or cavity my home base.

Different fortune had Thordskree.
Once a noble gentleman of striking expressions,
He gave up his looks to help some to be free,
More precisely, Your great-grandfather and his companions.

For in their Utter Love pursuit,
Your ancestors weren't that astute,
As they could not wait to get the loot
That later plagued and pierced their people mute.

Haunted and blurred their dreams at night,
The same that has happened to You,
Full of themselves in the fight,
Lost in that adoration while old they grew.

—I now understand better the cause
Of some of my people's reactions,
Said Dyosphir—Because
They knew about my forefather's distractions.

What I still don't know about
Is why you two didn't reach out to me!
Even knowing that I might have cut you out,
You should have had to come and see.

—You think we didn't attempt that too?
We've tried to warn Your advisors…—My, who?
—Well…that Your castle was about to fall through,
When they all laughed replying as in some—"Déjà vu…"

Plus Thordskree added—I still regret,
For there are things we never forget,
Like that moment we tried to protect,
But that ending I didn't expect…

—To you, I apologize for you too are my people.
Of your intentions, I should have been aware.
Nonetheless their ways are far from feeble,
And on my happiness, I've heard them swear.

And I swear too, upon my grave,
That the Joy Killers won't defeat us!
We are far away more brave,
Through our pain we've learned and plus.

Now help me out to understand,
Some more about *the Sphere*!
Is it material? Is it a land?
Is it something that I should fear?

—It is the most perfect shape
A man has ever seen,
Began the Child, describing,
What *it* knew it was another one's finding,
But *it* took for granted as if of *its* own it had been.

It's where all our dreams are trapped,
Right after they come to us for real.
Where everyone should be searching,
And battle themselves for that emerging,
Everything counts, even to steal.

Not a parallel reality,
Of questionable normality,
Where soon you will be
Trying to find Ivalisee,
While in search of the key
That might help us keep our serenity.

Where there is no pain that hurts,
More than the only one you bring,
Where no one can be saved from one's curse,
Even if that one happens to be a king.

—Have you ever been there, Child?
Asked Dyosphir, delaying his pace.
—No, I haven't; it's way too wild.
It answered, trying to hide the smile
That suddenly took over *its* face.

One of those, Dear Reader, we've all seen one time,
At least, You know—all covered up in grime,
Not so much innocent of guile
That no one could repeat or mime

And brings a few hundred lyrics
To our numbskulls or creative minds,
Yet once it gets possessed by spirits
That take control, making us cynics,
And therefore, slowly blind.

Now Thordskree suddenly wished he could see
Whatever made him raise his defenses.
Nevertheless, he did agree
To what brought to him his senses.

When the Child craned his finger,
Pointing behind our Prince,
Then looked down and seemed to wince.
The other two preferred to linger,
Feeling something they hadn't felt since,
A big dark sorrow that just grew bigger…

—Let's move along, this way!
We must hide now from the impostor.
Ordered the Child:—We cannot stay.
He's already here, the concealed monster…

Chapter VIII
Fears

— Behind the mountain's peaks...

VIII—①

Behind the mountain's peaks,
The gray was so intense
That the sun hid in eclipse,
Shielded by the moon's fence.

The Child they followed over the boulders,
Wishing it were cobblestone.
Still exhausted, they had to run,
Knowing that they were not alone.

A sense of weakness in the air,
Coming slowly out of nowhere,
Spread all over the valley in despair,
And in sadness beyond compare.

—We'll make camp here tonight!
Ordered the Child:—While there's still light,
Grab some wood, and make a fire;
Make sure it's not too bright.
The other two answered: "All right!"
And the three rested by the pyre.

At first sunrays, they built a raft,
For which they relied upon the Creature's craft.
Dyosphir felt His empty stomach.
Although He knew it was wrong to covet,
Still wondered, "How long will I have to fast?"

Again the Child heard our Prince's thoughts,
Besides the craving for His favorite sauce:
—Yes, I know; all that's alive mostly rots
And enhanced—Of some fine plants, we may come across.

The river currents led the way,
When the Child had to fight in silence,
With a sting that didn't go away
And kept threatening *its* balance.

Thordskree also felt the Killers' presence
And laid the Child down to rest.
The raft, just by coincidence,
Seemed to gain some conscience,
When it avoided the rocks by merging left.

—What's happening? We almost drowned?
—They are getting closer—said Thordskree.
The Child pointed out to the shore, to the ground,
Where they hit the bank under a tree.

—The Child is feeling them first.
Get *it* some water to satisfy *its* thirst.
Hurry up, Dyosphir, before things get worse!
I have a feeling that we are cursed.

The Creature had to take control
And gave *it* water for his console.
Together they dragged *it* into a hole
And waited for the Child to claim back his soul.

—We must go faster than the tyrant
Were the Child's first words after the swoon
—And find some safety, since here we haven't.
Let's walk at night, protected by the waning moon.

The three rambled at their pace,
One way slower than before.
Of those edible plants, they found no trace.
Steps got shorter, more and more…

Thordskree's thoughts were then dragged
Back to when he still had his looks,
His house, admirers, pets, and books,
Way back before he zigzagged.

For he was the first one for good,
To defy the enemy.
At the frontier once he stood,
Patiently awaiting his destiny.

As when the Joy Killers first threatened,
No one paid any attention,
For souls around *the Place* were getting
Fun and more fun in all its extension…

So he sat out there and waited
Alone for their strike, naked,
Sacrificing himself, unaided,
Expecting nothing and frustrated.

When they first hit him, it was like a spear,
Slashing the flesh of the enemy.
However, he stood his ground without fear,
For much it contributed to his chemistry.

Since by his side he had his globe,
Which blocked part of the spell, to spare,
The foolishness couldn't take control within a scope,
But his figure paid a price beyond compare.

After that everyone believed.
He was the proof that the Killers were real.
Alone with his globe the enemy he had blocked,
But the same hero left, as his wounds didn't heal.

He then wandered alone for long,
Too long before he could again be strong.
Nevertheless, all the things that went wrong
Were so many that wouldn't fit in a song.

It was when he became known as the Creature,
Much to do with his most disturbing feature,
Thenceforth he lost most of his vigor
And became a rare Utter Love Seeker:

Fears

A "real passion" disciple,
A faithful "affection" devotee,
A believer beyond the physical,
As avid for love as anyone can be.

Now again, my Beloved Reader,
Here are a couple of more words for You,
In case You decide to become a bleeder
And embrace one cause or, who knows, two,

Or leave Your footprints in the world,
If You want to put it that way.
Remember Thordskree, who didn't curl,
Nor quit and run away.

Be prepared for hurts and wounds,
As there might be a price to pay.
Yes, You could need a few stitches,
Trifling things that shouldn't affect Your spirits
Or Your will to go out and play.

For what You may find in the end
Would be something called joy, unless
You don't find Yourself unique,
For what I must state now that You are, so to speak,
More; I'd say it is not hard to guess.

As it shouldn't either be to understand
What happened after to those three men.
Well, as You know, things don't come always as we plan,
And we must fight with whatever falls in hand,
Like they did when our Prince also got slammed,
By the spell that almost hit Him in *Dyosphirland*.

—I feel dizzy; what's going on?
Gasped Dyosphir, drowning in sweat.
—We must hurry before our Mastron is gone,
The Child said—He is an easy one to get!

Thordskree again hurried to grab the globe
That he carried in his bag.
With no fingers, his claws would grope
(Remember that he never gave up hope?),
For they had no time to lag.

A sudden brightness flooded the spot,
Helping Dyosphir to improve a lot.
A wave of the spell He had caught,
But all three fought it with all they got.

Then the globe did bring more than a light,
For they heard at distance some squawk and chirping.
Some three birds that followed them in their flight
Fully stored the men's faiths by showing up in sight,
A sign of life when they thought there was nothing.

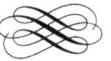

Our fellows regained some strength
And performed a gentle dance mimicking the birds.
Their feeble forces would now yield at length
Their drowned spirits cheered beyond words.

The Child shouted—Let's go find the Rose!
Dyosphir felt closer to Ivalisee;
A smile took over the Creature Thordskree,
A shy and internal one that only the soul knows,
And that could be, as I hope it be,
The meaning of a new hope, as far as it goes…

Now cheer up, Reader, for they're back again.
We're almost there. You don't lose Your faith!
Let's both toast to them, as they endured under pain,
One, to get what he wants, must also know when to wait.

Chapter IX
In Which Ivalisee Sings

In the meantime, beyond *the Sphere*,
Ivalisee waited for Dyosphir.
Not feeling him getting near,
She could not stop a tear.

So she sang to spook the fear,
A song of love and friendship
That she created while out there,
Tenderly whispering lip to lip:

—"Oh, wind of the Far East,
Have you seen my love at least?
Was he wounded by the Beast?
On his sanity did it feast?

"Oh, wind of the Far West,
Tell me he's still at his best!
For I've never rejoiced or slept,
Neither will put these bones to rest,
Relive the pain that's in my chest,
Unless I touch him with my affect.

"Oh, winds of all four corners,
Here I am at your orders.
Send a gust or just a breeze
To calm down this same old wheeze,
Appanage of true-love mourners.

In Which Ivalisee Sings

"Or just say you'll bring me my love,
Hovering on the back of any crow or dove.
Do you know that he is made of
All the skies and stars above?

"Oh, winds of the farthest corners,
Take this message in your storm.
Only you can go through borders
And pass the light upon this swarm.

"For all I need is his embrace,
Oh, winds of the farthest places!
Bring my love in all his grace,
As I can no longer wait,
Oh, please, oh winds of the farthest places."

While Ivalisee sang in despair,
She practiced her own calligraphy,
Finger pointed up in the air,
Writing and drawing on her creativity.

Blowing her poems in the Ether,
All above and beneath her,
As would do any other creature
Who knows his ways—a true believer.

Making imaginary plays
That would last for many days.
The most beautiful essays
Ending in winsome ways.

Petting dogs that didn't exist,
Swimming in lakes that weren't there.
The Sphere was made of a soft mist,
One too vague and beyond compare.

Smelling flowers that never breathed,
Feeling neither hot nor cold.
With dreams of freedom unfulfilled,
Forever young, endlessly old.

Sensing no thirst or hunger,
Without any symptoms of sickness,
No fatigue or tiredness,
Just the enduring unconsciousness of wonder.

When a need for somewhat to comb her hair
Struck her, she used her own long fingers.
You know, those curls that know they're there,
And man tries to forget, but memory lingers?

Fragrance? Oh yes, if you are doubting,
Any scent that would accent her skin.
So far, I hope your questions I've been answering,
The others I haven't—it's 'cause I ain't that keen.

In Which Ivalisee Sings

But I'm acute to say the following
About this tantalizing being,
Who yearned for her man and a wedding,
Even when all the odds were deceiving.

For their minds touched somewhere,
In a place beyond our comprehension.
One of those couples that refuse to share
The secret of all their affection.

If there's a real one out there, I wonder.
Somewhere to be found, a so-called secret.
I challenge it now to roar like the thunder
And therefore show itself to be convenient.

But if it decides not to sound its rumble,
Then we'll all assume that there isn't one.
So I shall declare that there's no secret in this couple.
Hence there is, in all the matters of love, also none.

Now let me take you back to our three heroes,
Who went out there to find some Roses,
Empty handed, without shields or arrows,
Regular mortals chasing their days down to zeros.

Trusting one another, as a bird trusts its wings,
For in their own minds there were no shadowy things.
Just a Prince and two striders riding boisterous winds
Of forbidden winters, in hopes of welcoming springs.

—Let's walk faster; daylight is here soon,
Said the Child, imposing the pace.
To spook the exhaustion, Thordskree started to croon,
But Dyosphir's legs simply gave up the race.

—I'm sorry, my brothers. I can't keep up with you,
I guess, at the end, I was just meant to fail.
All our Prince's doubts appeared to be true,
Of His vigor He was robbed, when His face became pale.

The Child and the Creature exchanged a glance,
One of those that mean more than a word:
—No worries, Master; we still have a chance.
We are not there yet, but we are moving toward…

It turns out that they had to carry Dyosphir
On the back of their shoulders, while feeding on older glories,
Until their strength quit and deserted,
Then along with their dreams of success it departed
To a distant place far away from their bodies.

The three rested their backs in the sand,
Next to one another along the riverbank.
Our eyeless Thordskree rolled over his body and wept,
For he knew that there was no fish to catch,
And in an epic-sob marathon, he sank.

In Which Ivalisee Sings

Feeling somehow responsible for their bad situation,
Way too lost in desperation,
As all around was just pure desolation,
The Child also released *its* frustration,
In the form of some self-mutilation,
For not being able to provide them any ration.

Now the three birds in the sky showed up again
And screeched somewhat in their native dialect.
Dyosphir still had the strength to wave back at them,
His final joy, plus His respect.

Our heroes just watched, for their vitality had gone,
The birds flying in circles, way up in the sky.
They knew it was over yet wanted to live on.
Nevertheless could do nothing but wait for the dawn
Or say farewell and then wait to die.

Yet up there they were, but sadly not that way high,
Along with all the reasons to ask: why?
Lush in attitude, humble in Aye,
Amid dried tears and all the time for good-bye:

—Here we are, my friends; I guess this is it.
I thought it would happen way differently.
Dyosphir was starting the endings when a hiss,
Coming out of the sky, as a robbed kiss,
Interrupted His thoughts of negativity.

They all stared at the tiny black spot
Falling down toward them in such haste
That the Prince, the Child, and the Creature could not
Follow its tracks, as it almost hit the first one in the face.

All three could not believe their eyes,
The two who had them and the one who did not,
As it came down from the sky something they sought,
(At one point will fall down anything that flies).
And one after the other the birds fell right in the spot,
Offering them their bodies, to our heroes' surprise.

The birds just decided to stop flapping the wings,
For they knew they were meant to nourish others.
Yes, in time, some can perceive one or two things,
When so many others just want to play fathers and mothers…

Chapter X
Ruby Vain Lake and the Trail of the Copper Beech Tree

— And the second concluded — It must be the Lake.   X - ⑰

In a life-span, it takes more than courage to survive,
Qualities like resilience and astuteness I've also embraced.
Yet, what the three birds did was more; it was divine,
And a word for them should be reserved.

Plus one more for every other beast too
As they are the purest of the pure;
Now try to imagine a world without them.
Yes, we'd all be doomed beyond cure.

Since we owe as much to purity,
As these birds to their wings, unfortunately,
Still, they accepted their last breaths merrily,
When we panic upon smiles and run screaming to therapy.

For in the beginning, we're all fur, scales, and feather,
Taking over the world for our own long pleasure.
Then, under pressure, finally comes the revelation,
The true find of our real big treasure,
One we've kept locked together
Along with our sorrows and procrastination.

Thenceforth, it will be too late,
Since it will be already empty, the plate,
Where You, my Reader, have eaten Your eternity
And vomited some kind of brevity,
Disguised in a one-day applause, for Your sake.

Don't be the one who looks around to his equal,
Thinking You're alone among so many people.
You're not a sparrow; Your alike, as well, is not an eagle.
Instead, go out there, and find Your reason!

As Dyosphir did three times, encouraging His friends,
After the bitterness that came upon them,
You should also check and restore those amends.
Before it's too late, allow them to see Your hidden gem!

—Let's go, brothers, we are almost there!
He said, as they hit the road, more enthusiastic than ever.
—Drop all your hopes now, my enemy; here I declare
That your peers and cohorts I won't spare,
As these two faithful friends guide me in this endeavor.

While I'm walking this white sand that will testify
My glory and of all my people's, which I shall restore,
I will make you a promise that I won't die
Before freeing all the ones whom I adore.

Thordskree zigzagged around his companion.
The Child again pointed out beyond *the Canyon*.
Our Prince had spoken with such passion,
Which triggered in them an uplifting reaction.

—Is that way our way, Child?—Dyosphir asked.
—Yes, it is—the Child avowed.
We must fly above it—he then joked,
And in a funny way, he added:

—One day a butterfly,
Of colored wings, just passing by,
Gamboled on His ears a warm good-bye,
And all His sadness suddenly died.

The Creature then joined in, mumbling some music notes
That reminded our Prince of an old shanty,
Women used to sing out of their tuned throats,
By the time He was around three.

—Thank you, fellows, it helps a lot,
Knowing that I can count on you.
I know now, but I wished that I knew
That sometimes a man alone can't untie the knot.

So keep on leading me, as you both have done so well.
I can recognize a good leader whenever I see one,
For he's the one who makes a man stop without tell,
And with no more than a gaze command him to run.

The three then walked away from the river,
Toward where the snow sometimes forgets to melt.
They passed under a thick lane of brushes when a shiver
Around their shoulders, necks, and heads was felt.

—What was this? Did you sense that shake?
The Child assented—My heart did ache…
More said the Creature—A silent quake.
And the second concluded—It must be *the Lake*!

—*The Lake*…what lake?—demanded Thordskree.
—*The Ruby Vain Lake*, between *the Canyon* and the *Trail*.
You'll then find the *Trail of the Copper Beech Tree*,
Once *the Lake* makes you feel weak and frail!

Our Prince then insisted—Ruby…Vain…why Vain?
—First, because it feeds on one's beauty,
And second, without causing any pain,
It'll steal it away, if one doesn't do his duty.

—And how does it know what's my duty?
—Once one—the Child shortened the pace and added,
—In there bathes, if the waters turn ruby,
Of one's beauty one won't be robbed.

—What about our Creature here?
Will his looks again appear?
Was his duty that unclear?
Would *the Lake* refuse to hear?

—*The Lake*, my Dear, works his way around *the Sphere*.
In comparison, it is powerless, beyond fear,
Though our friend Thordskree shouldn't even get near,
For it'll probably kill him, its atmosphere.

On the other hand, You, my friend,
Don't You want to know Your fate?
How it will be in the end?
Shall we both go there for You to bathe?

—My faith is bigger than the word of any lake,
The whisper of any mountain, canyon, or sea.
No matter what, I shall free my people from the stake,
And I will do the same with Ivalisee.

For no woman, man, or creature should bow
To any type of whispered conclusion.
Even if the odds against them are way low,
One must not fall in such delusion.

—Well spoken, Thordskree cheered,
Before he sensed a smirk on the Child,
Already walking ahead of him,
In a way somewhat grim,
And wished that he too had a mouth with which to smile.

Small figure, the Child was,
White skin, sleek voice, and callow eyes.
The Creature remembered the first day they'd met,
A day that he would never forget
And the instant he felt nothing but size.

Dyosphir, on the other hand,
Was way harder to understand,
Always a chief in command,
Eternally adored beyond His land.
Someone who had never been banned,
And to whom things always happened as He planned.

Now, once our heroes came up the rutted *Trail*,
The snow had already carpeted *the Canyon* and the *Peak*,
The air screamed the scent of ail,[13]
But their throats couldn't help but refuse to speak.

They hurried to tie a rope to one another,
In order to climb up and down,
Umbilical cord of the same old mother,
Which feeds both sister and brother,
And gives them birth in her chaste gown.

The rope did its job so well,
Preventing the three from another latter farewell,
That in the abyss the only thing that fell
Were their last doubts, escorted by a cheerful knell.

—Here we are—the Child sighed out of his lungs,
—The famous *Trail of the Copper Beech Tree*,
That from the dead the new awakening welcomes,
Breathing out the life that will sustain me!

The trees spread in a very orderly way,
Waving their gilded coppery manes,
Which turned to purple along the day,
Coloring the blood running in our heroes' veins.

Peace took over our Dyosphir fast.
In a sense of a journey halfway done,
The other two knew that He was the One.
No matter what had been His past,
This Prince should leave behind a son,
Who would rule as a true king, at last.

Sheltered by the oldest tree,
They closed their eyes, hummed by the falling snow,
The whitest one they had ever seen,
As if inside a womb, floating way too slow.

Chapter XI
Words and Gusts

Morning brought more than just light.
Some rays of hope accompanied the show,
One not to be missed, despite
All the ones You, My Reader, have caught so far, I know…

And a new day began for our Seekers,
To chase theirs and their ancestors' belief,
Questioning everything about the subject,
In hopes of getting some relief.

Despite the things they couldn't explain,
Like the Joy Killers' campaign,
To bring abstraction to one's heart again,
Unnatural torments and weights of pain,

They kept focused on their quest,
Refused to stop, take any rest.
However unreasonable it might seem,
No matter which way it would manifest,
Hope was always assumed at its best,
And work was held up by the team.

So they hit the road as fast
As they sensed success, at last,
Again, following the Child's footsteps,
With no hard feelings or regrets,
All eyes in the future, for yesterday was past.

Words and Gusts

Then a sudden cold wind and snow ruined their plans,
When, blowing from the East, froze their hands,
Some sort of claws, and extremities, and
Luckily, the Child had given the *Trail* a quick scan:

—There is a cavern somewhere in that direction,
It shouted in *its* deepest voice,
One that raised the following question:
—Do we still have a choice?

But *its* words were taken by the gust
To where all the words not heard will go,
A secret place they'll readjust.
In a rebellious ritual, You shouldn't trust,
As it might hurt the Love's flow.

For You, Reader, should never cross the borders,
Of Your greatest, precious, given gem[14]
Or run away from it when ditches and towers
Flood and rise below Your abdomen,

So if You're not sure about with what You're dealing,
You should instead keep quiet while searching,
But here is a hint: if You're not above stealing,
Snatch and move a letter to heal the plight You're feeling.

Unlike our friends, who did not grab
Or tricked or lured any to their trap,
When the Child decided to clap
And gave *its* fingers a quick snap.

The sound didn't help at all,
And away it went, following the words not heard.
Again, sounds also have a place where they crawl,
To wait until some noble cause points them toward.

Now here is a note to consider
About all the words' echoes and sounds unheard.
One should never abuse them, as their vigor
May lead them to fade away, if disturbed.

Unfortunately, that's what happened to our heroes,
Since these two allies both refused to show up.
And as there was no new plan in backup,
Their tired bones felt the call of the gallows.

Dyosphir and Thordskree followed one way,
While the Child got lost in the snow.
In *Dyosphirland* two dogs cried all day,
Howling: "Why alone did we let our Master go?"

I see a dark spot over there!
Pointed the Creature, grabbing our Prince's cloak,
He still held—We shall walk slowly and aware,
When a thunder loudly roared as he spoke.

Yet another wind gust made them fall,
And on their knees and elbows they had to crawl.
The slope had an opening gentle and small,
Which was not easy to get in, at all.

Nevertheless, they did so and made it.
Once inside, both leaned against the wall.
Dyosphir was glad that they didn't quit,
When the Creature let out an awful bawl:

—We lost the Child. The Child we lost!
We must go out there to get *it* back,
By any means, whatever the cost,
Only he makes up for all parts I lack…

But when Thordskree crawled back to the entrance,
A sudden gust brought down a wall.
That didn't allow him to finish the sentence.
Another raging uproar he was unable to control.

—The Child is stuck outside, Dyosphir!
He yelled, believing that the Child could hear.
—Do you still hear me, my dear?
My eyes are gone, but my heart shall tear…

—Do not say that, Thordskree!
Reacted our Prince—way differently than you, I see.
That we will find him, I guarantee.
Remember that the Child is more spirited than we!

Darkness instantly flooded the cave.
Dyosphir's words echoed inside the Creature's mind,
—Now let's find a way out of here. We're brave.
Getting your globe out of the bag would be so kind…

The globe lit a passageway,
Deeper inside the cave.
Both began to descend right away,
Over their heads feeling its cold wave.

—It's freezing down here, way more than outside.
I hope that the Child has found some shelter!
Thordskree led the way, but his thoughts he couldn't hide.
Nor could Dyosphir do anything better.

They walked as close to each other as they could,
But the ground was so rough that both stumbled all the time.
When the cold got too intense, our heroes considered a stop
And tried to make a fire, but there was no wood to chop.
Then, in no time, all changed; they'd have to start to climb.

—We must continue climbing, for we can't go back.
—There will be a way out ahead; one there must be…
Our Prince didn't speak out His best feeling,
Although in a miracle He couldn't help believing,
Though He was a faithful perception devotee.

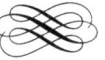

Surely, Friend, there'll be some chapters in Your lifetime
That You won't be trusting 'cause they don't rhyme,
Or somehow the stars and higher things will seem not to align.
Busy they are, healing wounds of many others and mine,
But one's convictions will change time after time.
Like certainties, also Your doubts are part divine.

Still, as the two heroes climbed inside the cave,
The temperature rose considerably.
Also, Your fears will go up and down like a wave
That dictates one's fortune vigorously.

Next, Dyosphir rested his back against the muggy wall
And slid down until it touched the ground.
His flesh felt the warmth, but that wasn't all.
As soon enough, He felt an urge to sprawl,
In a moment of joy, as if His core state He had found.

And as our Prince stared at the cave's ceiling,
Brightened by a dim light way too pleasing,
Delivered by the globe Thordskree was holding,
He noticed the little encrusted crystals gleaming:

—I had a best friend for a while…—He started.
We too used to lie on our backs at night
In a flat land, staring at the sky, inspired,
Pretending that all the stars were guarded
By us two, the Master and his Knight.

We made a lot of plans together,
Not just because our hearts were hanging high,
But also for the simple pleasure
Of just being there for what I've always wondered why.

I guess of time we kept losing track
(Oh, all that old innocent sweetness,
The anguish of being beardless…),
Before the day we lost contact,
May the night be my witness,
When he jumped into the unknown to never come back.

The Creature put down the globe,
Tried to speak out, but his urge was slurred,
For against those words there was no hope,
And that night no more voices in the tunnel were heard.

Chapter XII
The Flower Passages

— The Creature then sat beside him,
 Holding his head plus his own will to cry...

XII - ⑨

The Flower Passages

—There is light out there!
Echoed in Our Prince's ears,
Waking Him up from a nightmare
That seemed to be lasting a few hundred years.

He got up from the floor,
As fast as a tender snail
Runs away from the boiling water pot,
Before one throws in the kale.

Unless You prefer some bread crumbs and butter,
Sautéed in garlic, cut with a garlic cutter.
Not sure, Dear Reader, for it won't make them any smoother,
Though You can hear them squeal as You enjoy Your supper.

And eating was a thought that crossed His mind,
When Dyosphir walked toward the Creature to find
That the light was coming out from the ground,
Floodlighting odd roots growing on the wall of some kind,
Which He had never seen before in His lifetime,
As one could say that for too long He had been around.

—What do you make of this, Creature?
Have you ever seen anything of this nature?
He asked, staring up and down,
While Thorskree found himself somewhat astound
Before he answered—Well…I've never seen anything greater.

The cave's tunnel seemed to have no end.
As they both again began to ascend,
The roots got bigger, so big that they bent
With the weight of colorful flowers of great scent.

—The *Flower Passages* were real after all…
The Creature exhaled out of his maw.
—I've heard about them growing from inside the wall,
He continued, while running over the blossoms with his claw.

But their awe didn't last long,
Since our Prince suddenly fell to the ground.
Thordskree immediately sensed what was wrong,
As He could no longer come along,
With an eye movement, a gesture, or a sound.

The Creature then sat beside Him,
Holding His head plus his own will to cry,
Caressed His hair and forehead skin,
Then embraced His body in a deep, deep sigh:

—I must get to the root fast,
While He's still riding the waving blast,
Before all is forgotten, and at last.
No man or beast could tell the past.

The Flower Passages

So that any cute face or being that crawls,
Monsters with claws and scales; folks with a cause;
Ghosts with members able to climb walls;
Architects of songs, sounds, cries, noises, and calls,

Is able to organize itself in a way
That allows our story to be written in some lines
And be the matter of an old or new play
Performed in our backyard or at the *Epidaurus*[15] sometimes.

However, what the Creature forgot to mention,
In his apprehensive but acute outbreath,
Was another fact that needs our attention
And has nothing to do with death.

Something that is in general ignored,
By the one's so-called "short seeing."
Not suggesting he was one such being,
For eyes weren't something that were with his face adorned.

The real fact is what's usually forgotten,
So let's now take a look at the big picture:
It is true that our Prince hit the bottom,
But let's not forget about His people.

For they were the ones left behind
At the mercy of the Killers,
Condemned when their hearts, petrified,
Began to fall flat among other things it triggers.

Now, what would You have done instead, Reader?
Would You have been a follower or a leader?
I won't judge You; I was once a bidder,
When I swam the ocean just to be with her.

Yet our Prince had a tougher choice to make,
When compared with the one here speaking.
So let's root for Him not to break
And hope that all this has a meaning.

At least one that would make sense,
In the minds of those who worry,
There's an ocean of meanings, and it's immense,
Yet even bigger, if You're slightly blurry;

And please do not bring heredity[16] here
(A note for the ones who learn from their own mistakes).
There's nothing wrong with a Man who can't cross the frontier,
For his merit's greater than the impact he thinks it makes.

While the fog kissed the earth outside,
The body of our Prince in the Creature's arms reclined.
Though he couldn't hold it any longer, thus he cried,
But deeply he knew that there was more he could provide.

So he carried Dyosphir on his back,
Then slowly throughout the tunnel zigzagged,
Keeping himself on his track,
Quickly reacting to that tremendous drawback.

He did it for what it seemed like an eternity
And to spook unhelpful feelings often thought about the Child,
When they used to dine during the fall, wordlessly,
Way back then, by the time he could still smile.

Meals taken under leaves so gray,
Falling lifeless down all over,
That melancholy of a Sunday,
You can't fight because You're sober.

Under the lights of the candelabra,
Both bodies lost in such craving,
Bubbling up like molten lava,
Eating, drinking, and misbehaving.

—"My dear Child, where can you be?"
I swear I just heard now coming out of his maw
The sweetest lament of someone who refuses to grieve
His loved one, for he knew this time the thieve
Refused to show up lest break down the law.

So he would keep on carrying Dyosphir,
Until he ran out of strength,
A privilege of those who never quit,
And keep on taking hit after hit,
Before falling flat on the cement.

Nevertheless, they needed to eat,
For he could no longer stand on his feet,
But nowhere around was there a sign of meat.
That, yes, would have been a treat.
Hence Thordskree decided to sit
And try to feel our Prince's heartbeat:

—I will boil some flower leaves,
He prayed softly—for what it matters,
I kind of sense we're at the eaves,
Before all that counts suddenly shatters.

It has been said that they've the power to heal
Whatever is out there to be healed;
Out of them I would make our meal.
You must feel as hungry as I feel,
Regardless of the harm that might yield.

For I too shall live; it is my will,
Plus to save us all, before all of us I kill,
About knowing when to move fast or stand still,
I'll take my chances and await the bill.

It happened that our Prince woke up,
Right after the Creature slid down one flower petal,
Floating on a cold-water soup.
He wished it had been reduced to pulp,
With an accent of thyme and a handful of fennel.

The flower potion worked like a miracle,
And He was back—our Utter Love Seeker.
No, I am not trying to be satirical,
Yet I know you've assumed He had gotten weaker.

More I have to say for Your amusement.
Here is a good one, Reader, You may want to skip.
Do not wait to catch the best slip.
You should root for the finest movement;
Refrain to laugh at the ones who fall or trip,
As miracles You should start considering at this moment.

As I'm sure the Creature did,
Right after he pulled off another one.
I guess not being a "real passion" disciple is a bid
One should slay keenly with any sword or gun.

Chapter XIII
The Saying

Dyosphyr's fingers were like grape berries,
Long result of His life's soft wanderings,
His lips though were two cherries
You'd want to caress and other things.

His skin was pale like the sound of wind,
On a breezy morning over the steppe,
Cuddling the old red-leaved oak tree,
One late afternoon in the month of Sep.

His good manners were evident,
Although His confidence was delicate,
Some could perceive a celibate,
And, for all it matters, One way eloquent.

By the other token, Ivalisee
Didn't have such luck, You see.
Unaware of her location,
She struggled to find her identity,
While still upholding her sexuality,
Wondering if she was real or just a creation.

But she clung stronger to her belief,
Which happened to give her some relief.
That bitter taste of anguish,
Sweetened with that touch of standoffish,
Served in a silver bowl of grief.

The Saying

All by a generous bosom, framed,
Entrapped in a tiny waist unashamed,
Of some candid purity unexplained,
Full of lust—one self-contained…

Fantasizing about her man
And some remote cabin in the woods,
To hide as close as they can
Behind quilts of feathers and hoods.

Next to a riverbank of cold waters,
Where they could bathe and dry in the sun,
Crystal pure and occupied by otters
That accepted the presence of others
And played joyfully next to them.

Where they could sit and stare at trees,
Thinking about the breeze for a lifetime or two,
Without saying a word except to the bees,
Which provided the nectar for their lovers' stew.

A place where He would play her a lyre,
Built of wood bent on a pyre,
Strings made of her hair, the color of fire,
Daring songs about all the things He admire.

    Plus some others that I don't dare to tell,
    Because I esteem our Dyosphir very well,
      And His trust I will never sell.
  Those secrets I'll guard underneath my shell.

Likewise the Creature who didn't give out the codes,
For he never revealed what happened next inside *the Cave*,
  And when they ultimately arrived at *the Crossroads*,
      Once again beating up the grave.

—*The Saying*—twice mumbled Thordskree—*The Saying*…
    —*The Saying,* you said, asked Dyosphir.
      —Yes, *the Saying,* they weren't playing!
  —You mean *the Crossroads Saying*? Are we here?

    —Indeed, we are. We are, indeed…
      Our Prince took two steps back,
    As in front of Him it was way too black,
And answered—I doubt that this is what we need!

    —Oh, You have heard about *the Crossroads?*
Rumor has it, it is unmentionable around The Prince.
—Well, they did remember about to whom they owed,
Added Dyosphir—and should swear to me ever since…

  —Curious fact—interrupted the Creature,
    —That they told You about such a thing
  That is supposed to harm You, our Leader.
Therefore, more darkness upon us it will bring.

The Saying

—Your leader is but a man,
Who was cultured as part of some plan
And has been doing what he can
Until now, as his life had just begun.

—Well-said, my Dear Prince,
Big tribulations take greater measures.
You have my admiration ever since.
I too shall do…whatever smears Your pleasures.

Nevertheless, we must move on,
And not waste time with the ordinary,
You're the Commander; all the others are gone.
To find our way out is now necessary.

The Crossroads are ahead of us.
One of two passageways we must select.
Let's wish for good fortune, and plus,
On our options we must now reflect.

—Which are? Pardon my forgetfulness,
Said Dyosphir—It must be the illness.
Though I see the problem's enormousness,
I cannot merely voice out just some random wild guess.

—Well remarked!—Thordskree said,
—For this conundrum that lies ahead
Is too important to be misread.
We must take time and repose instead.

The two leaned over a big crooked root,
Right in front of *the Crossroads*, with no more delay.
The Creature went silently in pursuit
of the words in *the Saying* for the rest of the day.

As they spoke about having to decide
Between the two paths that stretched ahead,
While through one's own heart they both would guide,
They'd reveal and say what has never been said.

About what ought to bring the future,
Or the revelation of what had happened in the past,
To acquire the knowledge to endure
And help to find one's love at last:

"By the Crossroad, the paths would show
Two separate ways of reaching joy.
On the left you'll see behind,
While on the right you must remind
About what you should or not destroy.

"On that journey you should bring
The knowledge to help you find your present way;
If you see ahead, you can fix and resolve,
Though with the past you could prevent the unsolved.
Now go on and choose one, if you may!"

The Saying

—Are those the words?—hurried Dyosphir.
—How dim and brute they might appear
That my brain complains, so does my ear.
And why is the next step so unclear?
As the most ignorant Mastron lies here,
Exposed as a warrior without his spear.

—Be patient with others, my Dear Prince.
I am sure they did the best they could,
Invoked the Creature, who seemed to wince.
—Remember that Your parents were gone by Your childhood.

Nevertheless, You were the chosen one.
That's why we have made it this far.
The moon protects You, and so does the sun.
I think the final stretch might have begun
To get us out of where we are.

However, You now must hurry to choose.
With all due respect, I don't mean to abuse,
But as we have no more time to lose,
Which of the two shall we cruise?

—I wished it could be that simple,
Since I sense more of a debauched sprint.
As to me being the chosen one, I wrinkle.
It should have worked out like that, but it didn't.

—Please, Master, we mustn't allow those dark thoughts
    To pierce through us at this right moment.
    The work of the Killers goes on till it rots
Our hearts…but I now keel, awaiting Your endowment.

As Dyosphir looked at the two entrances once more,
    They appeared as dark as a hungry throat,
    About to devour all the beasts in the moat
    Of His joy, plus all the things He adored,
    On a long digestion of rotting organs that bloat,
    As the acids slowly help, letting out their roar.

—We will proceed with the tunnel on the right,
    He finally hissed like a driven snake.
    —Until death, I shall for my future fight.
Ivalisee and my people away from me, They won't take.

Chapter XIV
Hopes

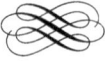

—I wasn't born a beast, but I shall as one die,
Uttered Thordskree in his utmost noble lament.
—To serve next to You was an honor, I can't lie.
May the worms spare the flesh of a being so repellent!

Nightfall took over (as if our friends were seeing one);
They wished! But there was no daylight whatsoever;
Inside the tunnel the dusk was like dawn,
And the spirits, well…those were lower than ever.

It was now our Prince's turn to cheer up Thordskree,
For that's what real friends do, said He:
—We must stay together. That's the key.
I'll comfort you now as you once comforted me.

While they carefully entered the chosen tunnel,
Dyosphir's entrails felt the need to rumble,
To spook the silence that, at once,
Took over without any trouble,
And muffled like a bubble,
The Creature's plights and slick grunt.

Furthermore to manifest
Its concerns and to confess
That it felt *the Sphere*'s slow disintegration,
Ivalisee's concerns and agitation,
Plus our Prince's people alone and in distress.

Hopes

Now, for our heroes this was treacherous ground,
And walking side by side, they started hearing a sound,
Coming from a place below, as they later found,
Which was a voice that echoed around.

They slowed down their footsteps while approaching,
What seemed like a sliver of a face
Attached to a standing body, smoking
And dancing, waving some ragged velvet cape:

—For whom do you cry? You once were asked.
Is there someone worth crying for?
I can repeat now, if I were tasked…
The voice sang as if masked,
Some familiar manners they've heard before.

—So where you're going? You once were asked,
For I want to go there too!
It persisted, unabashed,
—Say the right words, and I might guide you through.

The two friends shared a gaze
Of intense inquiry and silent amaze,
One of those that suggest some praise,
A little disbelief, but a thrill, always.

—Welcome to *the Gates of The Way*!—the voice stated.
—For both of you I have long waited.
—Is he the gate keeper?—the two friends debated.
—Will something happen to us that wasn't fated?

—The gate keeper I happen to be!
He declared in a deeper tone.
—To get where you want, you must go through me.
No one else can help you. I am the one!

And if you do, you will need a girl,
To show you where the root is.
Only delicate hands can unfurl
The secrets of the root in a little more than a whiz…

—We can try to say the words,
In hopes that you'll recognize
That there is no girl here, just two guys,
As all the others died in herds.

—Hurry, Master, it's Your time now!
Uttered again Thordskree with no delay,
—Only You can tell him how
Those words sound and clear our way.

—For whom I cry, I was once asked,
Held Dyosphir after a long, deep breath.
—I cry for *All the Lovers* who mask
Their feelings in life and are too proud to bet.

—To where I'm going, I was just asked.
Well, to the future! Seeking to outlive my past.
As if I will get there at last,
I shall tell you once through you I've passed.

The keeper dropped the ragged cape
And revealed *its* unique facial feature.
Thordskree's heart jumped out of its cage
And went sobbing outside the Creature.

For that face housed the most attractive eyes
Thordskree had ever seen.
Its lips were worth a thousand lies,
Leaving to guess around where they had been.

Its cheeks were finished with a ruler and a square.
The skin was the lightest color of ivory.
Black marbled and long was the heavy hair,
Falling through and around the neck, blithely.

—My dearest love!—mumbled Thordskree,
To Dyosphir's astonishment upon such reality,
As He still could not, actually,
Believe in what His eyes did see.

—Is that you, Child?—our Prince let out,
Unable to control the shout.
—Tell me what is this all about,
For I never again shall doubt.

—Yes, it's me!—the Child replied.
And for you two I have been waiting.
Dyosphir froze, petrified,
While still hearing Thordskree's heart panting.

—I could never have guessed,
Or for a while, I might have so,
Said our Prince, way too impressed,
With such a beautiful, flashing glow.

The Creature felt an urge to embrace the Child,
Though he knew that there was no time.
So getting closer, he sensed *it* as *it* smiled,
Overjoyed as when both had each other in their prime.

—Your answers have been accepted,
By *the Gates of The Way*'s Keepers' partners,
Myself in flesh, plus the ones above,
Stated the Child—the spirits of true love,
The eldest Utter Love finders.

Whom I shall join as soon
As I give you the Rose of Sharon's root.
To the Joy Killers, I shall myself sacrifice,
As it has been written not just once but twice.
Please refrain from words; be mute!

But Thordskree couldn't hold the pain,
And his tears he could neither contain,
Eyeless ones, unsalted, plain,
Running down, all over again,
Which he tried to hide, in vain,
Zigzagging back and forth, insane.

—Yet—muttered Dyosphir, comforting him,
—I can always come back to *the Crossways* and bring
The knowledge so that when I meet my current stream,
At this point in time I'll be able to fix this thing.

—Nevertheless—the Child enhanced,
We'll need someone to pull You back
From *the Sphere*, as there is no chance.
I'll send You there in advance,
Without a plan in case the Killers attack…

—Well, that one can be me!
Interrupted Thordskree.
—I can bring you back, and we will be free.
When the Child, nodding, added—I agree.

The three friends got out of *the Tunnel*
Through a hidden hole that the Child dug,
Entering Dyosphir's first future battle,
As easy as a worm gets out of the apple
And entwined in a group hug.

—Here it is, *the Valley of The Rose*!
Pronounced the Child proudly,
Waving *its* arm in some kind of cuddle as those
Who embrace their loved ones madly.

It was a vast flat land of small shrubs,
Dotted with buds of all colors in full blossom,
Which neither withered nor died in the autumn,
Eternally living in full spring without bugs,
Right across where all dreams will be forgotten,
Free of cyclones, earthquakes, and floods.

Thordskree then took a step back,
Keeping the Child's walk in sight,
To remember *it* by when all went black,
That the Child even had sun at night.

Chapter XV
The Plan

In *Dyosphirland*, two dogs couldn't keep quiet,
For they knew our Prince had little time,
And they felt His people closer to a riot,
Since the good dreams in *the Sphere* had long passed their prime.

Their heads grew heavier and heavier,
As days went by,
To a point where some could no longer stand up
And had to crouch and crawl in their waiting to die.

Covetousness and anger took over,
Among other talents; moreover,
The art of stealing drew closer,
While others got lost, like composure,

Plus pain, gaining a new place in the hierarchy,
Right between suffering and agony,
That tried to make ends meet,
Joining altogether with blasphemy
And later on banditry,
In a cocktail of gifts too hard to beat.

While at *the Valley of the Rose*,
The future heard the voice of those
Three friends who went to see ahead,
Willing to sacrifice two for one to wed,
Forgetting that the present forever goes.

The Plan

And there was no time to waste,
As the last leg hadn't yet been raced.
The Sphere was out there to be chased,
Doggedly, nonetheless, never fully embraced.

—You must learn, Dyosphir,
Held the Child, while in pursuit of the best bud:
—How to search within *the Sphere*,
As it can bog down Your judgment like mud.

Don't allow Your nightmares to corrupt
All the values You were taught.
Remember, *the Sphere* could often be unjust,
But if in Your good dreams You do trust,
You won't have to win the girl at any cost!

Believe Yourself, that's all You'll need.
Remember that Thordskree will bring You back,
No matter if You weep or bleed.
The rule is neither simple nor abstract.

You will have limited time once there.
Make sure to use it with judicious care.
Plus as Your hands and feet will both be bare,
Never ever body-fight, anywhere!

Only love should You pursue, once inside *the Sphere*,
That ought to debilitate the Killers' rear.
Therefore push them away from the frontier,
Letting in morale to come into Your people here.

Dyosphir's mind spun around too fast
For Him to grab His thoughts.
He had more questions than He could ask,
Yet they all got entwined in knots.

The Creature then came close to Him,
As if to say good-bye.
Nevertheless, his words came out dim
To a point where he couldn't avoid his cry.

And the three friends followed the Child,
Until *it* stopped next to the most vivid shrub,
Where *it* shouted—Yay, we're up!
As *its* lips sketched the brightest smile.

Its delicate hands then caressed the flowers,
The leaves, the spikes, and all the branches,
Amalgam of virtuous powers,
Way too daring to take chances.

Next, *it* whispered some bizarre lyrics,
To the perplexity of the other two,
Who wondered if The Child was talking to some dark spirits,
Such an unworthy thing for a Seeker to do.

The Plan

Still *it* picked some buds in full bloom,
Which freed the most pungent perfume,
Dispersing any hint of gloom,
And thanked for all the Roses' doom.

—What do You intend to do in case of withdraw?
Let out the Creature in an outburst of weakness.
—I can go back again to the tunnel after the thaw,
Reminded Dyosphir, not giving up to hopelessness.

But the Child heard them at a distance
And shouted out loud to their doubts.
Despite knowing their lives would change that instant,
The Sphere revealed all its brutes and louts.

—You two come closer; it's about time!
We shall gather under any *Bush of Dreams*.
One has to be found right away and in its prime.
Let's separate now into two teams!

Thordskree and our Prince went west
On what wasn't a hard or long quest,
Since the Child shortly found one at its best
And hurried the others to a test.

Where they would repeat all, *it* said,
About any adversity or threat
That could have Dyosphir misled
And kill our Prince and Ivalisee instead.

Later on, the Child cut all the Roses into pieces,
Smaller than an eyeball,
Then turned *its* back for some reasons
The others could not guess at all.

Suddenly stillness took over the *Valley*
In a way they didn't understand.
Our Prince and Thordskree looked at each other, sadly,
Knowing that things could easily get out of hand.

The wind ceased caressing their faces,
All the leaves in the shrubs, and its Roses.
Then a light breeze coming from higher places
Took over, bringing gusts of fragrant posies.

Next Thordskree dared to ask:
—Have we finally reached that moment?
Will this be it, my friends…
The point where our journey ends…?
As in some kind of last lament.

—It is not, my dear!
Jumped the Child, interrupting.
—We will be forever separated.
But I once had the man I was fated,
As before him I had nothing.

The Plan

The wind got stronger and louder,
Bringing along with it gushes of gigantic power,
And when it brought that massive shower,
Our Prince questioned if He had always been a doubter,
A weak man, some quitter, a coward,
Hiding behind high stonewalls in His ivory tower.

—Never!—shouted the Child, hearing His judgment.
—But You might have been tired of plenty,
Of playing hard day and night for Your amusement,
And now it happens that You're just feeling empty!

You have proven Yourself along this journey
In more ways than You might think,
Stepping forward when things were blurry,
Not complaining any time You were thirsty,
Lifting Your men off the ground when You felt them sink.

The three friends had to shout at each other,
Since the wind kept getting stronger.
Suddenly it roared like a loud peal of thunder,
Under the chosen *Bush of Dreams* that gave them cover.

That was when the Child turned to the Creature,
Now sobbing like an infant child,
—You were the noblest Seeker,
The most passionate lover, the best teacher
Anyone could ever find.

But now you carry this burden upon your shoulders,
Of bringing our Mastron and Ivalisee back from *the Sphere*.
You must drag them out if any fighters or soldiers
Of their past dreams dare to appear.

And place them where they belong,
Right next to His people;
Now, from this Rose you must cut the sepal,
Straightway feeding it to His dogs. Here, don't be wrong!
Next, you wait at the top of the steeple,
Humming loud His favorite song.

As the Child fed the Roses to Dyosphir,
Thordskree caressed the Child's face,
And then whispered, as our Prince slowly entered *the Sphere*:
—Welcome to Your unconsciousness; welcome to Your race.

Chapter XVI
The Sphere

The Rose's root potion didn't fail at all,
By the way it fooled the Joy Killers.
Our Prince entering *the Sphere* was as easy as a call
A mother swan makes to her newborn chillers.

Plus it was done in such a way
Some of You might relate to,
You lucky ones who don't need to call on Your sleep's dreams
For help to find Your truth.

Nevertheless, He had preferred to sail
Some troubled waters amber pale,
Humming shanties, drinking ale,
Lulled by the chant of the big white whale.

But that's not how it works, is it?
How about when fate gets in the way of a free spirit?
Tell me now, my Respectable Reader,
As I believe in the ways of merit,
You might relate to, if You've pushed it to the limit.
Go on and show it now, if You ain't no cheater!

Because, as You know, our Prince wasn't either one,
And despite all His flaws, He had never run.
Now, inside *the Sphere*, He'll have to fight
His unkind dreams, plus all the others in sight,
Since He won't stop until He's done.

The Sphere

And it didn't take them too long to show
How fast inside one they grow,
For no matter where He'd go,
His dreams and others couldn't wait to follow.

Although that was not the worst,
For soon enough some dared to attack.
Despite how loud He cursed,
They kept on going, never to retract.

Thus the first one was not as bad,
As the other that came after,
For some fellow who dreamed about going mad
Decided to chase a certain prince until death,
Waving a tongue-tearer of a scornful laughter.

Now guess who was the chosen one,
Of all the princes in *the Sphere*,
Who ended up taking the madman down with no gun
And fought him without His spear?

Despite what the Child had told Him that day,
When our three friends were at the *Valley*,
Well, our Dyosphir did indeed disobey.
Nevertheless, He didn't walk away.

Besides the fact that He had never a day of struggle,
Certainly not once ever gotten in trouble,
Always protected by the staff and His council,
From all He was sheltered, hovering inside a bubble.

Therefore, He kept on searching for Ivalisee,
Shouting her name out loud all around the *Dream's Sphere*.
I don't know, Reader, if You agree,
But that was not a bright thing to do, Dyosphir, dear…

As it woke up some really bad dreams,
Fallen hopes, and nightmares, to be precise,
Like His own, in which Ivalisee screams,
While being devoured by rats and mice.

And others like this one,
Some little girl dreamed about,
Really wicked, which freaked Him out,
Almost making Him stop His run:

In which all the beasts from the past,
Plus everyone dead,
In short, each living thing that has passed
Would await in their deathbeds.

Deep in the ground's entrail,
For any soul that passed by,
Elderly, young, of any race or style,
And pulled them down, whether they would laugh or cry,

The Sphere

To play hide and seek, way down below,
Cuddling, squeezing, holding them, embracing soft and slow,
Here and there competing in a body throw,
Nibbling on their eyeballs for all the eternity or so.

But again our Dyosphir didn't run away,
From that one or any other that followed.
Though He could have guessed who dreamed about the day,
Some prince and his lover in happiness wallowed.

After all He had to go through,
Like the moment it rained swords and knives,
Chopping limbs that were thrown in a giant barbecue
By some husbands, before they grilled their wives.

Plus another one I almost forgot about,
In which all our heroes were heading
To a feast of beer and trout
At Ivalisee and Dyosphir's wedding.

However, before that, He still had to find her; true,
When a fetid silence suddenly grew.
Well, *the Sphere*, Reader, is some place we all pursue,
Yet, don't misjudge it, as it can cruelly slay one too!

And the smelly silence then, little by little,
Became more pleasant and sweeter.
Next, He found this hint right in the middle
Of some familiar scent, so innocent and simple.

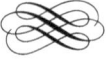

Dyosphir bounced back and forth, lively,
Trying to smell better here and there,
Then shouted—Yes, precisely!
For that was the smell of her russet hair.

He then followed that scent
As an edgy and hungry bear,
And on a rampage, He went,
Slicing into half anything, everywhere.

With a sword He had snatched before
Randomly off some murderer's hands,
Right after slashing his throat with vigor,
Avoiding the massacre of more lambs.

The Joy Killers could stop Him no more,
He felt less and less confusion,
As a result of the Rose's power that, somehow,
Helped Him in keeping His vow
And His feelings free from any delusion.

But not long after, He started feeling some trouble.
There was something wrong about *the Sphere*,
As if all His dreams had abruptly gotten blurry,
And He had to find her in a hurry,
Before it all suddenly would disappear.

The Sphere

Meanwhile in *Dyosphirland*, the Creature
Felt the wrath of our Prince, the Seeker,
Through one of His dogs, the leader,
And His killing craze at *the Sphere*, eager
To find, save, and finally be with her,
Despite what the Child said, the mind reader:

To never ever body-fight
Or try to bring the girl back at any cost,
As it had to be done right,
Under the menace of all being lost.

Though those words in our Prince's mind,
I mean, the Child's counsels for the attack,
Were nowhere to find,
As He had left them all behind,
Once He had sensed her hair and lap.

—Oh, Ivalisee, I'm almost there.
My love for you cannot be compared!
—Please come fast, my Prince, I'm scared,
As things are crumbling everywhere!

He then felt that He had to stop
And take a deep breath to think clearly.
For those few moments, He didn't chop
Off any heads as He was mentally blocked,
Sensing the Killers wounding His people's natures severely.

So He decided to climb up the tallest peak,
In order to adjust His mind and hear her voice clearer.
He did it so, though becoming very weak.
But it worked great, as her chant came nearer.

Toward where He ran faster than His legs could,
Rolling down as a dead rock,
Near the other side of the hill where, in shock,
He found Ivalisee at last for good,
Delicately humming as a nighthawk,
Or any other beautiful creature would.

She stared at Him like a statue,
Whose chest panted rhythmically.
A smile in the midst of her tears grew,
And mumbled—My love…at last you came to me…

Chapter XVII
Dreams

—Dreams sometimes hurt more than wasp stings,
Sighed the Creature to our Prince's dogs,
Calmly petting their furry skins,
At the top of the steeple, while fighting the odds.

Which didn't help that much,
Since the animals were way too agitated,
As they sensed our Prince's struggles
From the moment they had been separated.

But now, Reader, that Dyosphir had found Ivalisee,
Yet, to lose her, after all, what would that be?
Well, let's not forget that love must be pursued repeatedly,
Under the penalty of succumbing to a joy-killing spree.

Besides, she was still far from touching range.
Plus He knew that soon enough all that was about to change,
And while His wet eyes were stuck on her,
He suddenly felt something strange,
An endless echo that disarranged,
The chaotic harmony around *the Sphere*.

However, He couldn't care less,
About that or any other mess,
Since His blood was flowing way too fast,
Around places overly critical and enthusiast,
Inhibiting Him to ponder or process.

Dreams

Therefore, the two kept walking toward each other,
Floating in such an eternity of wonder
That the sudden roar of the loudest thunder
Didn't spook them from staring at each other.

He savored her graceful movements,
While she walked toward Him,
And lusted on her tumid breasts,
Lulled by their calling as in a summer hymn.

His heart He felt running wild,
About three feet away from her or so.
Obstructing Him from talking, He smiled,
In pure bliss, beguiled,
Forgetting to say: "Let's go!"

Nevertheless, *the Sphere* was far from happy,
And all its dreams it angrily converted to nightmares.
Even the one where these two fell in love madly
Was altered to another full of hates and despairs.

Jealous that such a love so deep
Could make them lose their sleep,
And stop dreaming or dream dreams incomplete,
Therefore its dynamic it was no longer able to upkeep.

For no other reason, whatsoever,
Not for pure enjoyment, peace, or pleasure,
It pulled the self-destruction lever,
Eager to swallow all dreams forever.

But our couple didn't even notice
What was happening around them,
Like some gigantic stillborn fetus
Preying on his own body once again.

Or the waterless ocean
Revealing lost treasures and dead fish.
The loathers all around shouting out their emotion
Or the crying rocks in agony, unable to quench their dumb anguish.

None of this for them was important,
Except the fact that they were, at last, together.
No man or dream could separate them, ever,
Or any *Sphere* in crisis with its reality distorted.

However, back in *Dyosphirland*,
The Creature couldn't contain the howling.
Our Prince's dogs weren't that hard to understand,
As they felt that the devastation in *the Sphere* was sprawling.

Plus they barked in such a way
That threatened the Creature's own integrity.
He knew that they could no longer obey
And fed them the sepal before releasing them prudently.

Thordskree ran to the top of the steeple straightaway
And hummed Dyosphir's favorite song throughout the day.
He then saw the skies' outbreak in dismay,
Crying hints of fire and shouting waves of gray.

The dogs barely made it into *the Sphere*,
Since chaos had mounted camp everywhere.
Though some Killer's troops hid themselves, paralyzed in fear,
Others battled the unbeaten unaware.

The Sphere hurled its rage against all,
No matter whether it moved or stood still.
There was no secret place for dreams to hide or crawl.
Nothing they could do would survive its will.

However, the dogs' loud barking
Opened up flanks in the battleground.
They easily passed on through everything,
Following their sense of smell all the way around.

Still in the midst of all this commotion,
They found tracks of their beloved Mastron.
At last, He had returned to their devotion.
I've never seen paws running with such emotion!

I witnessed their fangs drooling the sap of the miserable,
The greedy, the dejected, and the disgustful,
Which they left behind in a lethargic and atypical
Condition of inertia, eternally irreversible.

And their eyes were set on Dyosphir,
As if nothing else mattered,
While our Prince's sight was fixated on His dear,
Sparkling with fire, enamored.

He was about to kiss her,
When a giant mouth at a distance
Devoured every part of *the Sphere*,
At *the Sphere's* own insistence.

Ivalisee shuddered upon such an uproar,
But again she couldn't take her eyes off Him,
And when He was about to lean down to her,
The two dogs snatched our Prince by the limb.

And they ran as if they flew
Throughout the battlefield,
Avoiding rampages and riots,
Their Mastron's own insults,
Also disobeying His appeals.

Dyosphir cried and begged,
While being pulled out of *the Sphere*.
He cursed the Child and Thordskree,
Plus His dogs that were setting Him free,
But didn't acknowledge or save His dear.

Meanwhile in *Dyosphirland*,
His people celebrated hand in hand
The Killers' tumultuous disband,
Brought by the vanishing of *the Sphere*, and
As they no longer needed to stand,
Their own hearts again slowly started to understand.

While the dogs followed the melody,
Hummed by the Creature throughout the air,
They dropped Dyosphir successfully,
Next to Thordskree with all the care.

But He couldn't control His temper,
Until the Creature reminded Him of *the Crossways*:
—You can always go back, remember?
The left tunnel You then must enter.
Now go back with no more delays!

Dyosphir mounted the dogs hastily
And rode them trustworthily,
Up to *the Trail of the Copper Beech Tree* that patiently
Waited, hiding what could change our hero's destiny.

He galloped more than one day and night,
Wishing that all His life He'd been wrong in His pursuit,
Since He only foresaw "real passion" in sight.
Therefore in no way was He going to lose this fight
And change His Utter Love view.

But He held His judgment until arriving at *the Trail*,
Where He searched for the entrance in a frenzy and satirical
Performance that became no more than weak and frail,
Deeply believing in the ovation of a miracle.

The entrance, however, was nowhere to be found,
And our Dyosphir saw Himself fallen center stage,
Alongside His dogs, who in vain tried to lick the rage,
But lastly brought Him back, once again safe and sound,
To His *Place*, where the helpers calmed down His rampage
And assisted their Mastron in a sleep long and profound.

Later that day, when His people regained their joy,
Their now-free hearts chanted and celebrated with beer
Some shanties of love and of ships in convoy,
While all I wished was for a dream to come to Him clear.

Rhyme Scheme

I. ABAB
II. ABCB
III. AAAA
IV. AABAAB
V. AABBA
VI. AAAA
VII. ABAB
VIII. ABAAB
IX. ABAB
X. AAAA
XI. AAAA
XII. ABAB
XIII. ABAB
XIV. ABBA
XV. ABAB
XVI. ABAB
XVII. AAAA
XVIII. ABAB
XIX. ABAB
XX. ABAB
XXI. AAAA
XXII. AAAA
XXIII. ABAB

XXIV. ABAB
XXV. ABAB
XXVI. ABCCB
XXVII. ABCCB
XXVIII. AAAAAA
XXIX. ABAB
XXX. ABAAB
XXXI. AAAA
XXXII. ABAAB
XXXIII. ABAB
XXXIV. ABBABA
XXXV. ABAB

Note: This poem consists of seventeen chapters, with thirty-five stanzas each, totaling 595 verses. Each chapter of the poem follows the rhyme scheme shown above.

Endnotes

1 Egyptian sun god.

2 Assyrian and Babylonian deity.

3 "The Bride of Abydos," by Lord Byron.

4 Mariner, navigator, sailor.

5 Chinese green tea, also known as lucky dragon tea.

6 Constellation.

7 Type of song once commonly sung to accompany labor aboard sailing vessels.

8 Dolphins, sharks, and whales have no scales.

9 Sail.

10 A flat mass of ice (smaller than an iceberg) floating at sea.

11 God of medicine in ancient Greek religion and mythology.

12 The building at the *Asclepion* in *Epidaurus* where dream cures by enkoimesis are reported.

13 Aromatic bulb used as seasoning.

14 Love.

15 Ancient Greek theater in the Peloponnese region.

16 Genetics.

About the Author

Bruno A. Ribeiro is a Portuguese American writer and painter. Having studied fine arts in Lisbon, he moved to the United States in 2005 to fully dedicate himself to writing. He currently lives in Oyster Bay, New York, with his wife. *The Book of All Lovers* is his first published book.

www.ingramcontent.com/pod-product-compliance
Lightning Source LLC
Chambersburg PA
CBHW041619220426
43661CB00046B/1507